FUN-SCH

180

DiNoSaur

Learning GaMes & Poems

*Read, Write, Spell,
Draw & Color*

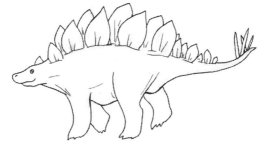

WriTten & ILLuStrated By ANNa MiriaM BroWN

The THiNKiNg Tree PubLisHiNg CoMpany LLC 2016

MY NAME:

MY FAVORITE DINOSAUR:

MY AGE:_____

DATE:_____

INSTRUCTIONS
FOR PARENTS OR TEACHERS:

1. Read each poem four times, pointing to each word as you read it. Many of the words are sight words that do not follow the rules of phonics. The child must be able to recognize each word visually.

2. Ask the child to repeat after you for the 3rd and 4th readings, the goal is for the child to memorize the rhyme.

3. Provide the child with colorful gel pens and one black gel pen.

4. Help the child to understand the instructions on each page. Sometimes the child will color a spelling word, write a missing word, complete a logic puzzle, color a picture or draw the missing part of a dinosaur. Sometimes the child will draw the dinosaur's food and habitat.

5. Write poems together in the back of the book. If the child is not ready to write, have the child dictate the poem or story, while you write it down. While you write you are being a good example to the child. Children learn best by seeing a good example!

TRICERATOPS

Triceratops, Triceratops
I look and I see,
How you eat
Green leaves from trees.

Triceratops, Triceratops
Do you like to play,
In the jungle,
On warm summer days?

COLOR ME!

Continue the Pattern

TRICERATOPS

Triceratops, Triceratops
I **LOOK** and I **SEE**,
How you eat
GREEN leaves from **TREES**.

Triceratops, Triceratops
Do you like to **PLAY**,
In the **JUNGLE**,
On **WARM** summer days?

Note to Parents or Teachers:
Read the poem one more time and ask the child
Point at, say, and color the special words with gel pens.

Draw my Food & Habitat:

Practice Writing

TRICERATOPS

Triceratops

Draw the Missing Part:

ZUNICERATOPS

Zuniceratops, Zuniceratops
I look and I see
How you eat
Leaves that are green.

Zuniceratops, Zuniceratops
I now can see,
That you like salad,
But I prefer cheese.

COLOR ME!

Continue the Pattern

ZUNICERATOPS

Zuniceratops, Zuniceratops
I LOOK and I see
How you EAT
Leaves that are GREEN.

Zuniceratops, Zuniceratops
I NOW can see,
That you LIKE salad,
But I prefer CHEESE.

Draw my Food & Habitat:

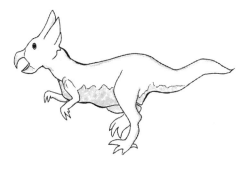

ZUNICERATOPS

Zuniceratops

Draw the Missing Part:

PTERODACTYL

Pterodactyl, Pterodactyl
Do you _____ to _____,
Through puffy clouds,
High in the _____?

Pterodactyl, Pterodactyl
In the sky so blue!
If I could _____,
I would _____ with you!

Draw my Food & Habitat:

PTERODACTYL

Pterodactyl, Pterodactyl
Do you love to fly,
Through puffy clouds,
High in the sky?

Pterodactyl, Pterodactyl
In the sky so blue!
If I could fly,
I would fly with you!

COLOR ME!

Continue the Pattern

Practice Writing

PTERODACTYL

Pterodactyl

Draw the Missing Part:

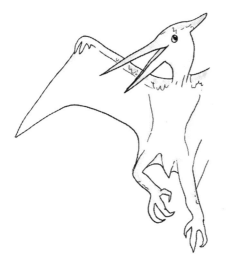

ALAMOSAURUS

ALAMOSAURUS,
ALAMOSAURUS
WHAT DO YOU EAT?
ARE FISH OR LEAVES
YOUR FAVORITE TREAT?

ALAMOSAURUS,
ALAMOSAURUS
YOUR NECK IS SO LONG,
YOU CAN REACH LEAVES IN
THE TREES,
AND SIP FROM THE POND.

COLOR THE WORDS & COLOR ME!

Continue the Pattern

ALAMOSAURUS

Alamosaurus, Alamosaurus

What do you _____?

Are _____ or _____

your favorite _____?

Alamosaurus, Alamosaurus

Your _____ is so _____,

You can reach _____ in the _____,

And _____ from the _____.

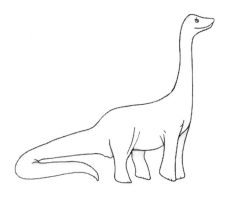

Draw the Missing Part:

ALAMOSAURUS

Alamosaurus

DRAW A DINO COMIC!

Allosaurus

Allosaurus, Allosaurus
You are very strong,
You have short arms,
But your legs are long.

Allosaurus, Allosaurus
Sun or shade?
Take a run in the sun,
Or a nap in a cave?

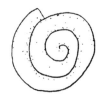

Draw my Food & Habitat:

ALLOSAURUS

ALLOSAURUS, ALLOSAURUS
YOU ARE VERY STRONG,
YOU HAVE SHORT ARMS,
BUT YOUR LEGS ARE LONG.

ALLOSAURUS, ALLOSAURUS
SUN OR SHADE?
TAKE A RUN IN THE SUN,
OR A NAP IN A CAVE!

COLOR THE WORDS
& COLOR ME!

Continue the Pattern

ALLOSAURUS

Allosaurus, Allosaurus
You are very _____,
You have _____ arms,
But your _____ are _____.

Allosaurus, Allosaurus
____ or _____?
Take a ____ in the sun,
Or a nap in a _____?

Draw the Missing Part:

Practice Writing

ALLOSAURUS

Allosaurus

DRAW ME!

ANCHICERATOPS

Anchiceratops, Anchiceratops
Are you having fun?
You play all day,
In the warm summer sun.

Anchiceratops, Anchiceratops
Where do you play?
In the sun, in the sand
Or in the jungle shade?

COLOR ME!

ANCHICERATOPS

Anchiceratops, Anchiceratops
Are y__ having fun?
You p__y all day,
In the w__m summer sun.

Anchiceratops, Anchiceratops
Wh__e do y_u play?
In the s_n, in the s__d
Or in the j__gle sh_de?

Draw my Food & Habitat:

ANCHICERATOPS
Anchiceratops

DRAW A DINO COMIC!

ANKYLOSAURUS

Ankylosaurus, Ankylosaurus
You have armored skin,
When you fight other Dinos,
I bet you win!

Ankylosaurus, Ankylosaurus
What do you eat?
Do you like veggies,
Or do you like meat?

Draw my Food & Habitat:

ANKYLOSAURUS

Ankylosaurus, Ankylosaurus
You have armored _____,
When you _____ other _____,
I bet you _____!

Ankylosaurus, Ankylosaurus
What do you _____?
Do you like _____,
Or do you like _____?

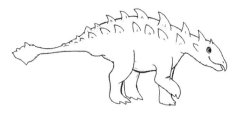

Draw the Missing Part:

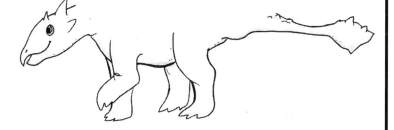

Practice Writing

ANKYLOSAURUS

Ankylosaurus

COLOR ME!

APATOSAURUS

Apatosaurus

Apatosaurus Apatosaurus
Tall as can be!
You are as tall
as the leafy trees!

Apatosaurus Apatosaurus
Do you like to eat,
Yummy green leaves,
From very tall trees?

COLOR ME!

APATOSAURUS

APATOSAURUS
APATOSAURUS
TALL AS CAN BE!
YOU ARE AS TALL
AS THE LEAFY TREES!

APATOSAURUS
APATOSAURUS
DO YOU LIKE TO EAT,
YUMMY GREEN LEAVES,
FROM VERY TALL TREES?

Draw my Food & Habitat:

APATOSAURUS

Apatosaurus Apatosaurus

_____ as can be!

You are as tall

as the _____ trees!

Apatosaurus Apatosaurus

Do you like to _____,

_____ green leaves,

From very tall _____?

Draw the Missing Part:

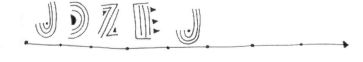

Practice Writing

APATOSAURUS
Apatosaurus

DRAW A DINO COMIC!

CRYPTOCLIDUS

Cryptoclidus, Cryptoclidus
Do you like to swim,
In the Sea,
With your friends?

Cryptoclidus, Cryptoclidus
What do you wish?
Do you wish for seaweed,
Or do you wish for fish?

COLOR ME!

BPASB

CRYPTOCLIDUS

Cryptoclidus, Cryptoclidus
Do you like to SWIM,
In the SEA,
With your FRIENDS?

Cryptoclidus, Cryptoclidus
What do you wish?
Do you wish for SEAWEED,
Or do you WISH for fish?

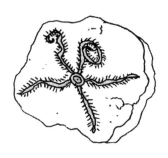

Draw my Food & Habitat:

CRYPTOCLIDUS

Cryptoclidus

Draw the Missing Part:

ARRHINOCERATOPS

Arrhinoceratops, Arrhinoceratops
Do you like to play,
In the jungle,
On sunny days?

Arrhinoceratops, Arrhinoceratops
Do you like to play,
By the river,
On cloudy days?

COLOR ME!

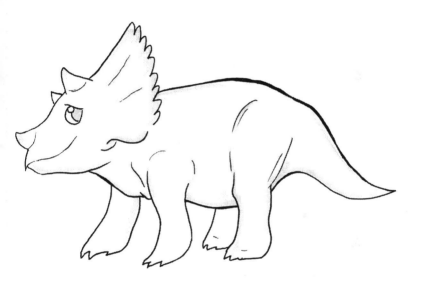

ARRHINOCERATOPS

ARRHINOCERATOPS,
ARRHINOCERATOPS
DO YOU LIKE TO PLAY,
IN THE JUNGLE,
ON SUNNY DAYS?

ARRHINOCERATOPS,
ARRHINOCERATOPS
DO YOU LIKE TO PLAY,
BY THE RIVER,
ON CLOUDY DAYS?

Draw my Food & Habitat:

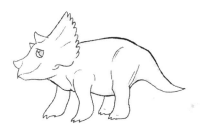

Practice Writing

ARRHINOCERATOPS

Arrhinoceratops

Draw the Missing Part:

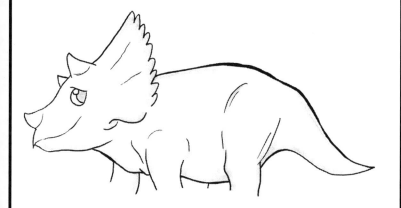

DILOPHOSAURUS

Dilophosaurus, Dilophosaurus
What's your favorite treat?
Do you run through the jungle,
Looking for something to eat?

Dilohposaurus, Dilohposaurus
When you want a snack to eat,
You will run passed the veggies,
Looking for meat.

COLOR ME!

DILOPHOSAURUS

Dilophosaurus, Dilophosaurus

What's your favorite _____?

Do you _____ through the _____,

Looking for _____to _____?

Dilohposaurus, Dilohposaurus

When you want a _____ to _____,

You will _____ passed the _____,

Looking for _____.

Draw the Missing Part:

DIMORPHODON

Dimorphodon, Dimorphodon
How far can you see,
When you fly
Through clouds and trees

Dimorphodom, Dimorphodom
Do you like to fly,
Through the jungle
Or through the sky?

COLOR ME!

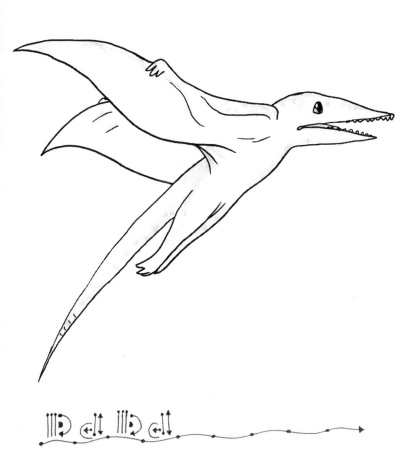

DIMORPHODON

Dimorphodon, Dimorphodon
How far can YOU see,
When you fly
Through CLOUDS and trees?

Dimorphodon, Dimorphodon
Do you LIKE to fly,
Through the JUNGLE
Or THROUGH the sky?

Draw my Food & Habitat:

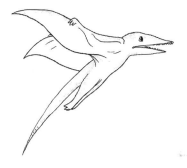

DIMORPHODON

Dimorphodon, Dimorphodon

How _____ can you _____,

When you _____

Through _____ and _____?

Dimorphodon, Dimorphodon

Do you like to _____,

Through the _____

Or through the _____?

Draw the Missing Part:

DIMORPHODON
Dimorphodon

DRAW A DINO COMIC!

DIPLODOCUS

Diplodocus, Diplodocus
What do you eat,
Are leafy greens
your favorite treat?

Diplodocus, Diplodocus
Can you reach,
The greenest leaves,
From the tallest trees?

COLOR ME!

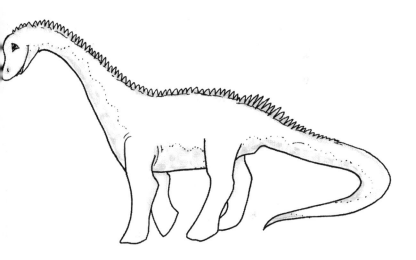

DIPLODOCUS

DIPLODOCUS,
DIPLODOCUS
WHAT DO YOU EAT,
ARE LEAFY GREENS
YOUR FAVORITE TREAT?

DIPLODOCUS,
DIPLODOCUS
CAN YOU REACH,
THE GREENEST LEAVES,
FROM THE TALLEST TREES?

Draw my Food & Habitat:

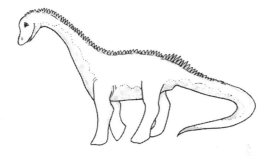

DIPLODOCUS

Diplodocus, Diplodocus
What do you _____,
Are _____ greens
your favorite _____?

Diplodocus, Diplodocus
Can you _____,
The _____ leaves,
From the tallest _____?

Draw the Missing Part:

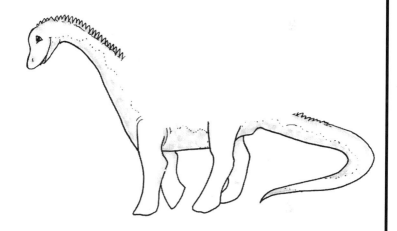

DIPLODOCAS
Diplodocas

DRAW A DINO COMIC!

ELASMOSAURUS

Elasmosaurus, Elasmosaurus
You are so sleek,
in the ocean,
Dark and deep.

Elasmosaurus, Elasmosaurus
you swim so fast,
through the sea,
seeking a snack.

COLOR ME!

ELASMOSAURUS

ELASMOSAURUS,
ELASMOSAURUS
YOU ARE SO SLEEK,
IN THE OCEAN,
DARK AND DEEP.

ELASMOSAURUS,
ELASMOSAURUS
YOU SWIM SO FAST,
THROUGH THE SEA,
SEEKING A SNACK.

Draw my Food & Habitat:

ELASMOSAURUS

Elasmosaurus, Elasmosaurus

You are so _____,

in the _____,

_____ and _____.

Elasmosaurus, Elasmosaurus

you _____ so _____,

through the _____,

seeking a _____.

Draw the Missing Part:

ELASMOSAURUS

Elasmosaurus

DRAW A DINO COMIC!

LEPTOSECADOPS

Leptosecadops, Leptosecadops
What do you eat?
Are leafy greens and berries
Your favorite treat?

Leptosecadops, Leptosecadops
What do you like?
Playing all day
But sleeping at night?

COLOR ME!

LEPTOCERATOPS

Leptoceratops, Leptoceratops
What do you <u>eat</u>?
Are <u>leafy</u> greens and <u>berries</u>
Your <u>favorite</u> treat?

Leptoceratops, Leptoceratops
What do you <u>like</u>?
<u>Playing</u> all day
But <u>sleeping</u> at <u>night</u>?

Draw my Food & Habitat:

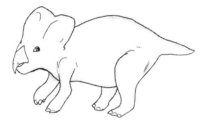

LEPTOCERATOPS

Leptoceratops, Leptoceratops

What do you _____?

Are _____ greens and _____

Your _____ treat?

Leptoceratops, Leptoceratops

What do you _____?

_____ all _____

But _____ at _____?

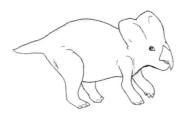

Draw the Missing Part:

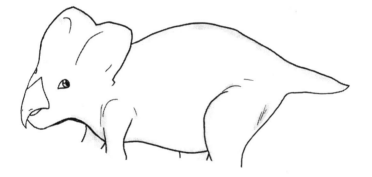

LEPTOCERATOPS

Leptoceratops

DRAW A DINO COMIC!

MACROPLATA

Macroplata, Macroplata
I look and see,
How you swim
Down in the deep.

Macroplata, Macroplata
I look and see
How you splash
In the sea.

COLOR ME!

MACROPLATA

MACROPLATA,
MACROPLATA
I LOOK AND SEE,
HOW YOU SWIM
DOWN IN THE DEEP.

MACROPLATA,
MACROPLATA
I LOOK AND SEE
HOW YOU SPLASH
IN THE SEA.

Draw my Food & Habitat:

MACROPLATA

Macroplata, Macroplata
I l__k and s__,
How you s__m
D___ in the d__p.

Macroplata, Macroplata
I l__k and s__
How you sp___h
In the s__.

Draw the Missing Part:

MACROPLATA

Macroplata

DRAW A DINO COMIC!

MAMENCHISAURUS

Mamenchisaurus,
Your tail is so long,
And like a cedar tree
Your neck is strong.

Mamenchisaurus,
What do you do?
Are leaves and fruit
Your favorite food?

COLOR ME!

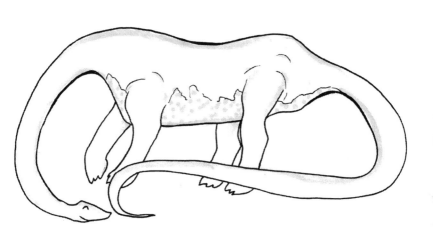

MAMENCHISAURUS

Mamenchisaurus,
Your t__l is so l__g,
And like a c___r tree
Your neck is s____g.

Mamenchisaurus,
What do you do?
Are l____s and f___t
Your favorite f__d?

Draw my Food & Habitat:

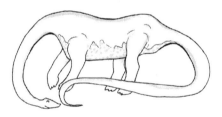

MAMENCHISAURUS

Mamenchisaurus

DRAW A DINO COMIC!

PATAGOSAURUS

Patagosaurus, Patagosaurus
Large, green and grey,
In the forests,
you like to stay.

Patagosaurus,
Patagosaurus
You like to play.
If you could talk
what would you say?

COLOR ME!

PATAGOSAURUS

PATAGOSAURUS,
PATAGOSAURUS
LARGE, GREEN AND GREY,
IN THE FORESTS,
YOU LIKE TO STAY.

PATAGOSAURUS,
PATAGOSAURUS
YOU LIKE TO PLAY.
IF YOU COULD TALK
WHAT WOULD YOU SAY?

Draw the Missing Part:

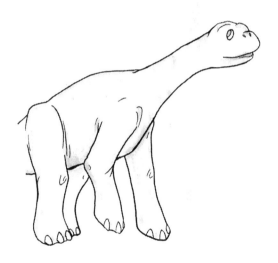

PATAGOSAURUS

Patagosaurus, Patagosaurus
Large, gr__n and g__y,
In the fo___ts,
you l__e to s__y.

Patagosaurus,
Patagosaurus
You l__e to play.
If you could t__k
what would y_u say?

Draw my Food & Habitat:

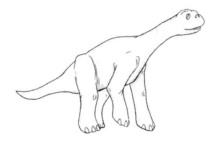

PATAGOSAURUS

Patagosaurus

DRAW A DINO COMIC!

PROCOMPSOGNATHUS

Procompsognathus,
You are sly and green,
When you hide in the bushes,
You cannot be seen.

Procompsognathus,
What do you do?
you search for meat,
Its your favorite food.

COLOR ME!

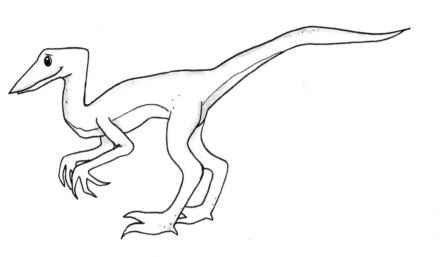

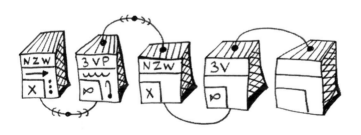

PROCOMPSOGNATHUS

PROCOMPSOGNATHUS,
YOU ARE SLY AND GREEN,
WHEN YOU HIDE IN THE BUSHES,
YOU CANNOT BE SEEN.

PROCOMPSOGNATHUS,
WHAT DO YOU DO?
YOU SEARCH FOR MEAT,
ITS YOUR FAVORITE FOOD.

Draw my Food & Habitat:

PROCOMPSOGNATHUS

Procompsognathus,
You are s__ and gr__n,
When you h__e in the b__hes,
You cannot be s__n.

Procompsognathus,
W__t do y_u do?
you s____h for m__t,
Its your f___rite f__d.

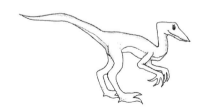

Draw the Missing Part:

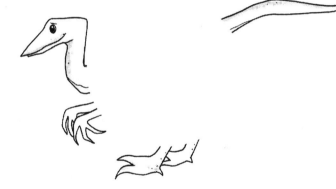

PROCOMPSOGNATHUS

Procompsognathus

DRAW A DINO COMIC!

PTERANODON

Pteranodon, Pteranodon
You fly so high!
Zipping and swooping
Through the sky!

Pteranodon, Pteranodon
Do you like to be,
Flying and gliding
In the breeze?

COLOR ME!

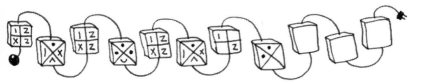

PTERANODON

PTERANODON, PTERANODON
YOU FLY SO HIGH!
ZIPPING AND SWOOPING
THROUGH THE SKY!

PTERANODON, PTERANODON
DO YOU LIKE TO BE,
FLYING AND GLIDING
IN THE BREEZE?

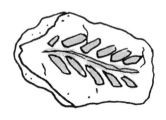

Draw my Food & Habitat:

PTERANODON

Pteranodon, Pteranodon

You _____ so high!

Zipping and _____

Through the _____!

Pteranodon, Pteranodon

Do you _____ to be,

_____ and gliding

In the _____?

Draw the Missing Part:

PTERANODON
Pteranodon

DRAW A DINO COMIC!

TYRANNOSAURUS REX

Tyrannosaurus Rex,
You are giant and strong!
You have short arms,
But your legs are long!

Tyrannosaurus Rex,
King of the beasts,
You stomp above
the tallest trees!

COLOR ME!

TYRANNOSAURUS REX

TYRANNOSAURUS REX,
YOU ARE GIANT AND STRONG!
YOU HAVE SHORT ARMS,
BUT YOUR LEGS ARE LONG!

TYRANNOSAURUS REX,
KING OF THE BEASTS,
YOU STOMP ABOVE
THE TALLEST TREES!

Draw my Food & Habitat:

TYRANNOSAURUS REX

Tyrannosaurus Rex,
You are g___t and s____g!
You have s___t arms,
But your l__s are l__g!

Tyrannosaurus Rex,
K__g of the b__sts,
You s___p above
the ta___st trees!

Draw the Missing Part:

TYRANNOSAURUS REX

Tyrannosaurus Rex

DRAW A DINO COMIC!

DRAW A DINOSAUR

WRITE A POEM ABOUT YOUR PICTURE:

DRAW A DINOSAUR

WRITE A POEM ABOUT YOUR PICTURE:

DRAW A DINOSAUR

WRITE A POEM ABOUT YOUR PICTURE:

DRAW A DINOSAUR

WRITE A POEM ABOUT YOUR PICTURE:

DRAW A DINOSAUR

WRITE A POEM ABOUT YOUR PICTURE:

DRAW A DINOSAUR

WRITE A POEM ABOUT YOUR PICTURE:

DRAW A DINOSAUR

WRITE A POEM ABOUT YOUR PICTURE:

DRAW A DINOSAUR

WRITE A POEM ABOUT YOUR PICTURE:

DRAW A DINOSAUR

WRITE A POEM ABOUT YOUR PICTURE:

DRAW A DINOSAUR

WRITE A POEM ABOUT YOUR PICTURE:

DRAW A DINOSAUR

WRITE A POEM ABOUT YOUR PICTURE:

DRAW A DINOSAUR

WRITE A POEM ABOUT YOUR PICTURE:

DRAW A DINOSAUR

WRITE A POEM ABOUT YOUR PICTURE:

DRAW A DINOSAUR

WRITE A POEM ABOUT YOUR PICTURE:

DRAW A DINOSAUR

WRITE A POEM ABOUT YOUR PICTURE:

DRAW A DINOSAUR

WRITE A POEM ABOUT YOUR PICTURE:

FUN-SCHOOLING WITH THINKING TREE BOOKS

FUNSCHOOLINGBOOKS.COM

Learning Should Be Delightful!

More Books By Anna Miriam Brown

My First Fun-Schooling JOURNAL
For Princesses & Ballerinas

Anna & Sarah Brown
Count & Color
Just for Girls

Fashion Dreams 1800 - 2030
TIME TRAVEL HISTORY
Fun-Schooling Curriculum Journal

Anna Miriam Brown ... Age 13
To Wear or Not to WEAR?
A Teen Girl's Guide to Getting Dressed
A Motivational Coloring Book

Made in the USA
Columbia, SC
22 November 2024